Mercy

Marcie Schneider
Michelle Borquez
Sharon Kay Ball

The Freedom Series
Created by Michelle Borquez

AspirePress
Torrance, California

Abortion to Mercy

© Copyright 2013 God Crazy/Bella Publishing
Aspire Press, a division of Rose Publishing, Inc.
4733 Torrance Blvd., #259
Torrance, California 90503 USA
www.aspirepress.com

Register your book at www.aspirepress.com/register
Get inspiration via email, sign up at www.aspirepress.com

All rights reserved. No part of this publication may be reproduced, stored in a retrieval system, posted on the Internet, or transmitted in any form or by any means without the prior written permission of the publisher. The only exception is brief quotations in printed reviews.

The views and opinions expressed in this book are those of the authors and do not necessarily express the views of Aspire Press, nor is this book intended to be a substitute for mental health treatment or professional counseling.

All Scripture quotations, unless otherwise indicated, are taken from the Holy Bible, New International Version®. NIV®. Copyright © 1973, 1978, 1984, 2011 by Biblica™. Used by permission of Zondervan. All rights reserved worldwide.

Scriptures marked "NKJV" are taken from the New King James Version. Copyright © 1982 by Thomas Nelson, Inc. Used by permission. All rights reserved.

Printed in the United States.

Contents

Chapter 1
Marcie's Story 7

Chapter 2
Bible Study 19

Chapter 3
Steps to Freedom 85

The Authors

Marcie Schneider knows what it's like to hide the deep, dark secret of abortion. God slowly and tenderly led her to a place of healing and freedom as he turned her mess into her message. Marcie desires to share with others who know this secret pain that allowing God to help heal them will set them free.

Michelle Borquez is a sought-after speaker and writer whose passion is to equip hurting women to break free from their pain, finding their freedom in Christ. As the spokesperson for Beth Moore's national TV special, "Living Well," Michelle knows the challenges Christian women face. She has worked as a consultant for the American Association of Christian Counselors and as a counselor at a crisis pregnancy center. Her books include *God Crazy, Overcoming the Seven Deadly Emotions*, and *The YOU Plan: The Christian Woman's Guide to a Happy, Healthy Life after Divorce*.

Sharon Kay Ball is a licensed professional counselor and a mother to three children. In addition to her private practice, Sharon is a staff counselor at her church. Her own personal experience with suffering, the daily grind of single parenting, and counseling her clients has given Sharon tremendous compassion and insight for those dealing with life's tragedies and trials.

Chapter 1
Marcie's Story

By Marcie Schneider

My best friend Sonja went with me to confirm what I already knew. Hearing the words, "It's positive," stirred feelings inside of me that I'll never forget.

I was sixteen and so scared. I worked up the courage to tell my parents, and the decision was made for me to have an abortion. It wasn't really my idea, but I sure didn't argue with it. The only person I really remember showing me any mercy or trying to discuss other options was my stepdad Jim. It's interesting now to look back at how I didn't think he cared at all about me. Nothing could have been further from the truth.

I wouldn't say I was neglected as a child, but I don't remember a lot of family time either. My parents divorced when I was four and my sister Michele was three. Mom and Dad both remarried and added half-siblings to the mix. Michele and I lived with my mom, stepdad, and half-sister Melinda. We went to my dad's house every other weekend until my stepdad was transferred to Colorado. I was nine years old when we moved, and until then my "happy place" was wherever my grandfather was. I loved spending time with him. When I was eleven, he died of a sudden heart attack. It was the saddest day of my life. Soon after his death, my mom moved us back to Texas so we could be closer to our family.

That's when the trouble began. In seventh grade, I started hanging out with a group of friends who liked to party. We drank alcohol when we could, and we definitely weren't concerned with sexual purity. We weren't actually having sex, but we were doing everything else. By the time I was fifteen, I lost my virginity at a party to a good friend

> Sex made me feel loved and wanted.

who was also a virgin. Believe it or not, it was just a game. Everyone was cheering us on to "do it," so we did. I knew what I was doing was wrong, but I got attention for it. Sex made me feel loved and wanted.

At sixteen, I was facing the consequences of my choices, leaving an abortion clinic literally empty inside.

Still, even the abortion didn't stop me from seeking love in the wrong ways. I continued to have sex and became pregnant for the second time, less than six months after my first abortion. This time I had a friend who was also pregnant, so we went to the abortion clinic together. This experience was very different from the first one. I remember everything about that day. I remember looking at the doctor's face, and I remember that he never spoke a word. I remember how it felt looking around the cold, impersonal recovery room and seeing the rows of beds occupied by girls and women like me. I remember the nurse who went from bed to bed, making insensitive comments and jokes.

By this point, I had convinced myself that I was pretty much a loser. I wanted the "good life," and I wanted to start making the right choices, but in my mind I was so far gone that it was just too late. I knew the good kids would reject me, and even if some didn't, I would never fit into their group. I felt I was forever marked as a slut who had no chance of ever being accepted by the "good" people again. I felt dirty and worthless. I had become a Christian early in my life, and I knew that God loved me and could forgive me, but I also knew how other Christians my age treated people like me. I was not about to put myself through that humiliation. I decided to stay bad and learn to deal with it.

> I felt dirty and worthless.

When I became a senior in high school, I reconnected with a guy who had graduated early, gotten a job, and now lived in his own apartment. I hated life at my house because I was grounded all the time and couldn't get through a day without fighting with my family. So I packed some clothes and moved in with him. When I didn't come home the first night, my mother called his apartment looking for me. I did not talk to her. I almost felt good about making her suffer. I wanted her to be sorry I was gone.

I finally called my mom several days later to tell her that I wasn't coming home because I had gotten married. This marriage wasn't about love, but it did feel like a fresh start.

Once I was married, it was "okay" to get pregnant. So I did, and gave birth to my beautiful daughter Britni when I was eighteen. I wouldn't trade that day for anything in the world; however, my dream of creating the perfect little family was far from the reality I was living. After only a year of marriage, my parents paid for my divorce.

Britni spent a lot of time at my mom's house. I wasn't a terrible mom, but I wasn't the kind of mom Britni deserved. I was still a teenager and still trying to figure out life and find love. I put my selfish desires ahead of her so many times. I loved her very much, but I was desperately seeking a relationship that would make me feel complete. I wanted to be loved, accepted, and adored by someone.

I had several relationships over the next few years. Some were serious and some not so serious, but most of them included sex. At the age of twenty-four, I once again headed for an abortion clinic. I remember sitting there, thinking to myself, "Is this really my third abortion? Maybe it's my fourth." I honestly could not wrap my mind around it. Each time I had an abortion, I buried the emotional pain deep in my soul. I also subconsciously buried the reality of what abortion was and that I was killing my own babies—three of them now.

> I buried the emotional pain.

This was the hardest to deal with because the father of this child was Marc, whom I later married. Marc and I went many years without ever discussing this issue.

Abortion to Mercy

Soon after Marc and I married, we became pregnant again. This time we chose life and we had a precious son Brock. We bought our first home and started a new business. Finally my life was good. It was just like I had always imagined. I had a great husband, a home, a daughter, a son, a dog, and even a new minivan in the driveway. Marc accepted Christ as his savior a year into our marriage, I rededicated my life, and I signed up to teach Vacation Bible School. We had a church, a Sunday school class, and Christian friends. You know, a perfect life, right? Not so much.

Over the next several years, God began to do a work in me that I did not see coming. I clearly heard God speak to me at a ladies' retreat when I wrote the word "anger" on a piece of paper and threw it away. I committed to get rid of my anger even though I had no idea where it was coming from. I really didn't recognize how deeply I had damaged my spirit in those teen years. God was so gentle in the way he led me down the path of post-abortion healing. Everything I had spent years trying to forget was all about to emerge, but God was faithful to hold my hand each step of the way.

> God was faithful to hold my hand.

Peeling back the years that covered a multitude of sins was extremely painful, but there was no way for me to completely heal without getting to the bottom of the pit. He showed me people in my life I needed to ask for forgiveness as well as those I needed to forgive. I was broken, truly repentant, and finally restored. Every now and then I still find a little leftover piece of some junk in my life. It still hurts to clean it out, and sometimes I'd rather start stuffing again, but then God reminds me of his faithfulness to forgive.

> "See, this has touched your lips; your guilt is taken away and your sin atoned for."
> —Isaiah 6:7

He also reminds me of his love for me.

> "May the Lord direct your hearts into God's love and Christ's perseverance."
> —2 Thessalonians 3:5

My past sin of abortion not only took the life of my unborn children, but also took away parts of my own life. It killed my spirit as the depression and anger continued to build up over the years. Many other sins and strongholds got lodged in the cement I was forming around my heart to protect it from any more pain. God began to chisel away at my hardened heart, and I felt him pour peace into my soul that I had never felt before. God tugged at my heart for a long time before I finally started letting him in.

Marcie's Story

My heart had learned how to turn off my emotions when I needed to and mastered how to keep anyone who triggered any emotion in me at an arms' length. But since my healing process began, I have seen my heart change time and time again. Recently, I spent a lot of time with my dad Bill as he went through chemotherapy and radiation for a very rare and aggressive cancer. I'm so thankful that God gave me the courage and strength to open my heart to build a relationship with my dad. As I continue to allow God to renew a steadfast spirit within me, I know there will be many more victories in my life like this one.

"Create in me a pure heart, O God, and renew a steadfast spirit within me. Do not cast me from your presence or take your Holy Spirit from me. Restore to me the joy of your salvation and grant me a willing spirit, to sustain me."—Psalm 51:10–12

Abortion to Mercy

Chapter 2

Bible Study

By Michelle Borquez

Marcie's story brings back the same memories—and the same shame—I felt as a young girl going through the horror of an abortion. There has been nothing in my life quite as painful as the memory of my own abortion. It was too painful to bear. I couldn't even imagine myself having done such a thing. I had buried the memory of it. So it was a surprise to me to find myself walking through healing years later. God, in his infinite wisdom and grace, had found a way to lead me to my healing.

In an effort to give back and redeem myself, I applied to work at a local pregnancy center, thinking that helping others would rid me of my painful memory forever. The clinic's director said that in order to counsel those who have been through an abortion, I would have to go through post-abortion counseling myself. I thought that because I had buried this memory and asked forgiveness I had been healed. But it wasn't until going through the counseling that I realized how tender that place in my heart really was.

As difficult as it was to face the pain of my abortion, to walk through it and overcome it was a journey to freedom I would never trade. I can talk about it today without pain—not without regret, but without pain—because I truly know that the Lord has forgiven me and released me from it.

The memory, combined with the loss, can be so overwhelming. Yet God is in the business of healing memories. He is in the business of gently peeling back the layers of our hard hearts in order to open us up and do the surgery necessary to heal us, to mend us, and make us new. Every morning when we wake up, his mercies are made new.

> "Because of the Lord's great love we are not consumed, for his compassions never fail. They are new every morning; great is your faithfulness."
> —Lamentations 3:22–23

How beautiful it is to walk in the freedom Christ brings through forgiveness. I pray this Bible study will lead you down a path of healing, and you too will be set free and able to walk in the purpose God has for your life. He has something so special for you in all of this. Ask him today what it is. Before we even begin, ask him what he desires you to receive.

Abortion to Mercy

(If you want, you can write your prayer here.)

Forgiving Yourself

Are you allowing the guilt, the memories of your abortion to overtake you—to consume you?

Sometimes one of the hardest people to forgive is yourself. It's almost easier to forgive others. We play the video over and over in our mind of all our mistakes, all our failures, and we hold ourselves in contempt.

Forgiving can only take place supernaturally. In our humanness, our

From Marcie's Story

"[My abortion] killed my spirit as the depression and anger continued."

ability to forgive is limited. We can easily justify holding ourselves in this place of contempt for a lot of reasons:

- "I am not worthy of forgiveness."

- "If anyone knew what I have done they would never love me or accept me."

- "I have gone too far this time. I could never be forgiven for such a sin."

- "I was a Christian when this happened. God could never forgive me because I knew it was wrong."

These are all lies the enemy works every day at convincing us of. It's the mind war that goes on in our heart every day. To believe Jesus could love us so very much that he would forgive us for such a sin is almost difficult to believe. This is where our faith to believe is necessary. We may think faith is just something we need to do great things or see miracles, but it also takes a determined

Bible Study

faith to believe Jesus could forgive us of such a sin as abortion—and to forgive ourselves of such a sin. Yet by faith we come, we bow before him, we lay our lives down, we repent as Marcie did, and we ask him to come in and heal our heart.

You may be thinking, "Michelle, you have no idea what I have done, what I have been through, or the wrongs I have committed."

My answer to you comes straight from God's Word:

> "But God demonstrates his own love for us in this: While we were still sinners, Christ died for us"
> —Romans 5:8

Read that verse again.

According to this verse, when did Christ die for us?

_____

_____

_____

_____

_____

_____

So then, when did Christ die for you?

_____

_____

_____

_____

_____

Christ died for all sin, not just some sin. He came and he gave his life so we can walk in freedom knowing that it's not by our own works or our own ability, but by the grace afforded to us by the precious blood of Jesus. So you see, faith comes in believing God's Word to be true for you; not just for others, or for those who appear to have it all together, but for the sinner, the downtrodden, the ones who have failed, who have walked away from him. He has died and given his life so that they may be saved; so that you may be saved and forgiven.

He goes on to say:

> "Nor can the gift of God be compared with the result of one man's sin: The judgment followed one sin and brought condemnation, but the gift followed many trespasses and brought justification."
> —Romans 5:16

Our faith comes in receiving the gift of forgiveness, freely given, so that you might be redeemed and restored and so others will see Jesus in you and the power of his healing hand.

> "And God raised us up with Christ and seated us with him in the heavenly realms in Christ Jesus, in order that in the coming ages he might show the incomparable riches of his grace, expressed in his kindness to us in Christ Jesus. For it is by grace you have been saved, through faith—and this is not from yourselves, it is the gift of God—not by works, so that no one can boast."—Ephesians 2:6–9

What is the difference between a gift and something that you've earned or paid for?

_____

_____

Bible Study

_____
_____
_____
_____
_____
_____
_____
_____
_____
_____
_____

Hearing about God's forgiveness may be the easy part, but actually allowing these words from God to transform your heart and mind can almost seem impossible. Recognize that forgiveness is often a process. Sometimes it can happen quickly, but sometimes what has happened to us cannot be processed so easily. You may have allowed your heart to become hardened due to the sin of your abortion or the things that brought you to the place of having an abortion.

I had a hard heart. My heart was not open to God for many years after my abortion. I was so angry, but didn't really know at whom; partly at myself I'm sure, and partly at God because of other heart bruises I had incurred along life's way.

From Marcie's Story

"I buried the emotional pain deep in my soul."

Ask the Lord, as Marcie did, to begin to peel those hard layers away, one by one; to go into the deep recesses of your heart and begin to find the areas that need healing. For most of us, we will not be able to grab on to our healing instantly. It's truly a life-long process. But in time, when you think of your abortion or hear of someone who has had an abortion, it will not prick your heart the way it used to. You will have compassion, but the guilt and shame will not come on you any longer because you have found your freedom in Christ.

Read this passage from the Psalms:

> "The Lord is compassionate and gracious,
> slow to anger, abounding in love.
> He will not always accuse,
> nor will he harbor his anger forever;
> He does not treat us as our sins deserve or
> repay us according to our iniquities.
> For as high as the heavens
> are above the earth, so great is his love
> for those who fear him;
> As far as the east is from the west,
> so far has he removed our transgressions
> from us."—Psalm 103:8–12

Abortion to Mercy

Which words caught your attention as you read this?

Bible Study

Remember that this Psalm is not just for others—it's for you. Try reading it again; but this time with a personal touch mixed into it. Add "me" or "my" in the verses below:

"The LORD is compassionate and gracious, slow to anger, abounding in love.
He will not always accuse _____, nor will he harbor his anger forever;
He does not treat _____ as _____ sins deserve or repay _____ according to _____ iniquities.
For as high as the heavens are above the earth, so great is his love for _____ who fear[s] him;
As far as the east is from the west, so far has he removed _____ transgressions from _____." —Psalm 103:8–12

I had a very hard time getting beyond my abortion. For years after, if I just heard the word *abortion* or saw something on TV related to abortion, I'd cry. I thought I'd never have children because I felt so undeserving. But God is not a man that he will bring judgment and make you pay (John 3:17). He sees. He does understand all the fear, the anguish, and the pain related to what you have gone through. For me, I was afraid. My parents were in ministry and I did not want to bring shame on my family. I thought my dad would never forgive me or ever talk to me again. Years later when my mom found out, it was not easy for me. She was so sad because she had lost a grandchild. I know that my child is in heaven and one day I will see him or her and be able to ask forgiveness.

One of the exercises I did in my post-abortion counseling was to write a letter to my unborn child asking forgiveness and saying things I would want to say. It was very healing for

Bible Study

me. It took me a while to be able to do it. It really put a face to what I had done; it was important to do so. I needed to realize the magnitude of my sin, and then to realize the magnitude of God grace in my life.

You may not be ready to write a letter just yet. God is okay with that. You write one, if and when you feel led to, but in your heart, say the things to your child you would want to say so you can release yourself from the hurt and pain. Say it to God and to your child. No one has to know but them.

From Marcie's Story

"I really didn't recognize how deeply I had damaged my spirit."

I also felt the Lord asking me to write a letter to myself. It had only one line in it, but it was repeated over and over again:

I forgive the girl of my past.

This was one of the most important things I did. I had the hardest time forgiving myself because I didn't feel I deserved it. None of us "deserve" to be forgiven. We are forgiven simply because of Jesus dying on the cross so we can be reconciled with him.

Is God prompting you to write a letter at this point in your journey? If so, pause and write down everything you need to say.

_____

_____

_____

_____

_____

_____

_____

_____

Bible Study

Abortion to Mercy

Bible Study

In counseling one day, God revealed a beautiful word picture to me. I was praying with my counselor and he was asking God to show me the Lord's grace and mercy in my life. I had lived with the deadly emotion of shame for years. I was enslaved to it and it was affecting my choices in life. I wanted so badly to get beyond it, and had even believed the lie that it was good for me to live with it so I could stay humble. The picture God showed me that day, set me free forever.

I saw a diamond as brilliant as the sun. In its brilliance I saw nothing but perfection. It was absolutely flawless, and almost difficult to look at it because it was so beautiful. In that moment I saw a gushing river of blood flowing over it. The river was so thick, so strong, but through the river of blood, I could see this diamond shining brightly.

This is what God said to me during this prayer time: "Michelle, when I look at you,

I see the most beautiful, flawless diamond shining brightly. I don't see your flaws, your failures, or your sins because you have been forgiven, and I now see you through the blood of my Son."

I realized in that moment that I had been holding myself in contempt based on my own set of laws and perceptions of how I looked at myself. I was not seeing myself through the eyes of God, but instead through my own eyes that see imperfection and the ugliness of my flesh.

What lies are you believing about yourself that are keeping you chained and enslaved to the bondage of shame and guilt?

_____

_____

_____

_____

Bible Study

Four Big Lies

Lie #1

I am not worthy of God's forgiveness.

Truth #1

"Therefore, my friends, I want you to know that through Jesus the forgiveness of sins is proclaimed to you. Through him everyone who believes is set free from every sin, a justification you were not able to obtain under the law of Moses."— Acts 13:38–39

According to these verses, who makes this forgiveness of sins possible?

_____

_____

_____

_____

_____

Bible Study

To whom is forgiveness of sins proclaimed?

_____

_____

_____

_____

_____

_____

_____

How many sins are we set free from?

_____

_____

_____

_____

_____

_____

There is no sin and no person who is not able to come to Jesus and ask forgiveness of their sin. Forgiveness means the slate is clean, the debt is cancelled, and there is no more record of it. You are free. Receive it, so you can no longer walk in the chains of shame.

Lie #2

You must pay for your sin.

Truth #2

You may know in your head that Christ died and took your sin away, but still you cannot stop believing the lie, the message the enemy is telling you every day, and you hold on to it because it's a way of punishment and helps you feel better about what you did. The truth is that there is nothing you can do to make up for your sin. Christ died for this very reason. We cannot atone for our own sin. It is not possible no matter what you choose to do. So holding on to your shame is only prolonging the arrival of the beautiful life

Bible Study

God has awaiting you. His desire is for you to be free so you can walk out his purpose for your life.

> "All have sinned and fall short of the glory of God."—Romans 3:23

> "In [Christ] we have redemption through his blood, the forgiveness of sins, in accordance with the riches of God's grace."—Ephesians 1:7

Attempting to atone for your own sin is attempting to do the impossible. We, in and of ourselves, cannot do enough or perform enough to remove our sin. Only asking for forgiveness and receiving God's grace in our lives removes the sin. This is truth.

> "If we confess our sins, he is faithful and just and will forgive us our sins and purify us from all unrighteousness."
> —1 John 1:9

Have you asked for forgiveness? Are you still trying to "pay for" what you've done—by beating yourself up about it or by trying to do enough good things to make up for it—instead of accepting God's gift of forgiveness? Journal your thoughts now.

_____

_____

_____

_____

_____

_____

_____

_____

_____

_____

Bible Study

Lie #3

My sin is just too great for God to forgive.

Truth #3

It's true that God is a holy and pure God, but he can handle our sins. We are—as I described in the beautiful picture God gave me of the diamond with no flaws—made holy and righteous through the blood of Jesus.

> "In you, Lord my God I put my trust. I trust in you;
> do not let me be put to shame nor let my enemies triumph over me."
> —Psalm 25:1–2

Jesus has made us clean and when we put our trust in him, when we truly believe the promise he has given in his Word, then we are able to flourish and live out the purpose he has for our lives.

Bible Study

> "Who shall separate us from the love of Christ? Shall trouble or hardship or persecution or famine or nakedness or danger or sword? ... No, in all these things we are more than conquerors through him who loved us. For I am convinced that neither death nor life, neither angels nor demons, neither the present nor the future, nor any powers, neither height nor depth, nor anything else in all creation, will be able to separate us from the love of God that is in Christ Jesus our Lord."
> —Romans 8:35–39

Are there things in your past that you feel can separate you from God's love? Write them down now in the spaces provided.

_____ will not separate me from the love of God that is in Christ Jesus my Lord.

Abortion to Mercy

_____ will not separate me from the love of God that is in Christ Jesus my Lord.

_____ will not separate me from the love of God that is in Christ Jesus my Lord.

_____ will not separate me from the love of God that is in Christ Jesus my Lord.

_____ will not separate me from the love of God that is in Christ Jesus my Lord.

_____ will not separate me from the love of God that is in Christ Jesus my Lord.

_____ will not separate me from the love of God that is in Christ Jesus my Lord.

Bible Study

Nothing will separate you from the love of God. Nothing is too big for God to forgive.

Lie #4

I cannot handle looking at this sin because if I do, I will not be able to accept myself and God will not accept me either.

Truth #4

This lie is based in fear. To live in fear of facing what we went through and truly recognizing it as sin is a fear of ultimately being set free. As long as we remain in the fear, we are unable to release the sin and move beyond it. It's right where the enemy wants to keep us. As long as he can keep us living in the shame and guilt of our sin and keep us in denial of it, he can keep us in a place of bondage.

> "Your faith should not be in the wisdom of men but in the power of God."
> —1 Corinthians 2:5 NKJV

It takes faith to open your heart and allow these secrets to be removed. Imagine holding your hands up, cupping them into a small bowl, and then throwing them into the air and releasing what is in your hands up to God.

Now write down on a piece of paper all that you are holding in your heart. Don't leave anything out. Take that paper, place it into your cupped hands and lift it over your head. Say to the Lord aloud: "Lord, I release this to you. I no longer want this secret to remain inside of me and as I release it to you, I ask that you would begin to do the necessary surgery to heal my wounded heart. Thank you for your forgiveness. I receive it today. In Jesus' name, amen."

Abortion to Mercy

Lord, I release this to you:

Bible Study

> *From Marcie's Story*
>
> "God was so gentle in the way he led me down the path of post-abortion healing."

So my sweet friend, how are you looking at yourself? Do you see yourself as God sees you? Have you set yourself free from the chains that once held you? I pray so.

Now that the chains have been broken, are you ready to break down the walls too?

Breaking Down Those Walls

When we go through heart bruises in our lives, it's easy for us to begin to put up walls around our hearts. Eventually we begin to shut people out, and not only are people not able to get to us, but God is not able to penetrate our hearts either.

The loss we encounter through abortion and the shame and guilt that accompany it, can stay with us forever—if we allow it to. Now that we have discussed forgiving and letting go of shame, let's go deeper in our healing and begin to look at how carrying shame and guilt has affected you.

Bible Study

Ask yourself:

- ❧ Have I felt unworthy and unable to step out into the purpose God has for my life?

- ❧ Has shame and guilt kept me from truly opening up my heart to my marriage partner or my family?

- ❧ Has shame and guilt kept me from volunteering at church with children or with teenagers?

- ❧ Has shame and guilt kept me from forming intimate relationships with others?

- ❧ Most importantly, has shame and guilt kept me from truly opening up my heart so I can encounter an intimate relationship with Christ?

As you read those questions, what were you feeling? Journal what's in your heart right now.

_____

_____

_____

_____

_____

_____

_____

_____

_____

_____

When we self protect, when we form a fortress around our heart and do not allow anyone to move through it, we are left to our own wisdom and tend to lose sight of the path God has for us. Our hearts can easily become bitter and full of mistrust if we do not allow our heart bruises to be healed. Like any wound, if not treated correctly, it can become infected and possibly be deadly. Heart wounds that go undetected do the same. They become infected and bring death to our soul if we do not deal with our healing. God's desire for us is to run free—to no longer be bound up with chains.

> "It is for freedom that Christ has set us free. Stand firm, then, and do not let yourselves be burdened again by a yoke of slavery."
> —Galatians 5:1

When our hearts are hardened, we are unable to show God's love to people. We are unable to be his hands, his feet, and to love with his heart. Jesus calls us to love, to have mercy and compassion, and to give these gifts away. When we are so bound up, we stay stuck, unable to move forward and embrace a future, and unable to let go of a past that continues to haunt us.

Jesus asks us to lay our burdens down so the weight we have been carrying is lifted and we are free to truly walk in the freedom he has for us. This freedom includes a future free to love and give love to others.

Asking God to give us his heart of abundance—his heart of grace and mercy—enables us to begin to step into things that we once thought we were not worthy of. We are worthy because he has made us worthy, not because of anything we have done or not done. Understanding that

> *From Marcie's Story*
>
> "I felt [God] pour peace into my soul that I had never felt before."

Bible Study

we have value regardless of our past mistakes is essential.

To love him with reckless abandonment and to run free in the purposes he has for us is the life he intended for each one of us. Suddenly we find ourselves having his heart for those who feel unworthy. With this amazing freedom from sin that we experience, we desire to give it to others.

Choosing to have God's heart is a decision we make daily. If we don't choose to have God's heart in each of our situations, it's easy to let our circumstances rule over us. We continue to lean toward unforgiveness, rather than accepting his perspective. Choosing to have his heart and to see ourselves through his eyes is what we base our foundation and value on. So his truth tells us who we are.

Abortion to Mercy

The messages we have been listening to all these years say:

- ❧ You're not good enough.

- ❧ You're not worthy enough.

- ❧ You're not pretty enough.

- ❧ You're a bad person and cannot be forgiven.

These messages are based in lies. In order to truly walk in freedom, we must focus our heart and mind on truth. If we can accept that God accepts us, we can embrace the beautiful joy he intends for us.

What messages are keeping you from allowing God to pour himself into you?

_____

_____

_____

Bible Study

You've heard the lies. But what's the truth? The truth about who you are comes straight from God's Word. Here's what we know about those who have chosen to put their trust in the Lord:[1]

- You are **forgiven**.

    *"In him we have redemption through his blood, the **forgiveness of sins**, in accordance with the riches of God's grace that he lavished on us."*
    —Ephesians 1:7–8

- You are **reconciled** with God.

    *"Once you were alienated from God and were enemies in your minds because of your evil behavior. But now **he has reconciled you** by Christ's physical body through death to present you holy in his sight, without blemish and free from accusation."*
    —Colossians 1:21–22

- You are **rescued**.

    *"For **he has rescued us** from the dominion of darkness and brought us into the kingdom of the Son he loves, in whom we have redemption, the forgiveness of sins."*
    —Colossians 1:13–14

- You are **redeemed**.

    *"For you know that it was not with perishable things such as silver or gold that **you were redeemed** from the empty way of life handed down to you from your ancestors, but with the precious blood of Christ."*— 1 Peter 1:18–19

- You are **bought** with a price and **belong** to God.

    *"Do you not know that **your bodies are temples of the Holy Spirit**, who is in you, whom you have received from God? You are not your own; **you**

were bought at a price. Therefore honor God with your bodies."
— 1 Corinthians 6:19–20

- You are **known** by God.

  *"God's solid foundation stands firm, sealed with this inscription: 'The Lord **knows those who are his**.'"*
  —2 Timothy 2:19

- You are **chosen** by God.

  *"For **he chose us** in him before the creation of the world to be holy and blameless in his sight."*—Ephesians 1:4

- You are **justified** before God.

  *"For all have sinned and fall short of the glory of God, and **all are justified freely** by his grace through the redemption that came by Christ Jesus."*
  —Romans 3:23–24

Bible Study

- You are **accepted**.

    *"Accept one another, then, just as **Christ accepted you**, in order to bring praise to God."—Romans 15:7*

- You are **saved**.

    *"Since we have now been justified by his blood, how **much more shall we be saved from God's wrath** through him! For if, while we were God's enemies, we were reconciled to him through the death of his Son, how much more, having been reconciled, **shall we be saved through his life!**"—Romans 5:9–10*

- You are **alive**.

    *"But because of his great love for us, God, who is rich in mercy, **made us alive with Christ** even when we were dead in transgressions—it*

is by grace you have been saved."
—Ephesians 2:4–5

🕊 You are **free**.

> *"Jesus said, 'If you hold to my teaching, you are really my disciples. Then you will know the truth, and **the truth will set you free.**'"*
> —John 8:31–32

🕊 You are **sealed** by God.

> *"Now it is God who makes both us and you stand firm in Christ. He anointed us, **set his seal of ownership on us**, and put his Spirit in our hearts as a deposit, guaranteeing what is to come."*
> —2 Corinthians 1:21–22

Bible Study

No Longer Victim but now Victorious!

Our continued effort toward self-protection only keeps us in a place of isolation and gives opportunity for the enemy to continue giving us the same messages about ourselves over and over again.

God sees and knows your heart; there is nothing hidden from him. We were made for relationship, and any authentic relationship begins with an open heart. We all long to be loved and accepted, not just by the Lord, but by others as well. I hope you now feel that you can begin the journey to open your heart up to those around you, and begin to love and live again.

> "So do not fear for I am with you; do not be dismayed for I am your God. I will strengthen you and help you; I will uphold

you with my righteous right hand."

—Isaiah 41:10

Have you felt as if you were not worthy, not good enough, based on your abortion? For years have you lived with this secret, telling no one? How has this affected your ability to be victorious in your life?

_____

_____

_____

_____

_____

_____

_____

_____

Bible Study

_____

_____

_____

_____

What perspective have you had of yourself until now?

_____

_____

_____

_____

_____

_____

_____

_____

> *From Marcie's Story*
>
> "I was broken, truly repentant, and finally restored."

My hope is that through hearing Marcie's story and mine, and seeing and hearing all God has for you—forgiveness, grace, mercy, and love—that your mind-set about who you are has shifted.

My prayer is that you are able to feel that you can walk with confidence, knowing that you are loved and adored by God himself.

Moving beyond a place of guilt and shame can be easier to say than actually to feel. It can seem so much easier to run and hide and keep those places in our heart hidden from God and others so we don't have to feel the pain. But moving beyond the place of being a victim of pain, shame, and guilt is what it takes to truly be victorious. Allow yourself time to heal. It's okay to let God heal your heart little by little. It doesn't have to be all at once.

When I accepted Christ at age twenty, I had already encountered many heart bruises, including the abortion. It would be many years before I would begin to deal with the pain of what I had walked through. Over the journey of my life, the Lord has slowly healed the broken pieces and redeemed each one. I am no longer enslaved to fear, shame, or guilt. There are no words to describe what it feels like to walk in such freedom and to truly know I am loved unconditionally and accepted by the Lord.

If God were to come in and heal us from everything at once, I believe it would crush us. Instead, he slowly awakens us to the areas of our life that have not yet fully surrendered to him. In his loving, patient way, he continues to grow us and change us as we begin to use our freedom to heal others.

Only when we become tired of playing the victim in our own story are many of us willing to reach for our victory in Christ.

When we continue to walk as a victim:

- We are anxious and stressed.
- We have a continued feeling of worthlessness.
- We feel insignificant and insecure.
- We feel unaccepted by God and others.
- We feel a constant sense of hopelessness.
- We feel unloved and are unable to give love.
- We feel used and unable to be free with our gifts and talents.
- We feel depressed.

Bible Study

- We feel uncertain about our relationship with God.

- We are unable to accept truth.

- We reject and renounce the truth in God's Word, instead walking according to our own knowledge.

Truth—God's truth—sets us free.

To walk in victory we must choose to:

- Embrace God's truth.

- Speak God's truth.

- Will his truth in our lives.

- Act on this truth.

- Become this truth.

When we are walking in victory:

- We are confident, but not arrogant.

- We are competent, but not controlling.

- We are significant, but not ego driven.

- We are successful, but our value is not based on this success.

- We are secure, but use our influence for good.

- We are worthy, but understand that worthiness comes from the forgiveness we have found in Christ.

- We are loved and accepted because of the sacrifice Christ made for us.

As long as we choose to remain a victim—not willing to exchange our heart for his, or our life for the life he desires to give us—then our hands remain gripped on the wheel, unable to let go and let God drive.

When we try to get our needs met apart from Christ, his truth, and his ways, we are walking according to our flesh. This leaves us in a place of weakness, feeling unfulfilled

Bible Study

and unable to give our heart away to others. We are shut down inside.

My heart is for you to walk in the victory Christ brings us through his forgiveness and through his Word so you can truly walk in the purpose he has for you. Yes, he does have a purpose for you! And a plan to prosper you!

> "For I know the plans I have for you," declares the Lord, "plans to prosper you and not to harm you, plans to give you hope and a future."
> —Jeremiah 29:11

You had an abortion, but you don't have to let the abortion define you. You don't have to let the abortion keep you in a place of being a victim any longer. You are not a victim; you are victorious through Christ. You are made new. Your sins have been forgiven. You are loved. You are accepted. You are free.

If you continue to struggle with your acceptance in Christ, look to his Word daily. Here are some Scriptures to get you started. I suggest making a pin board, or even a white board is fine. Put the board up in a place where you can see it every day. Every time you struggle, read these Scriptures aloud:

> "Yet to all who did receive him, to those who believed in his name, he gave the right to become children of God."
> —John 1:12

> "For he has rescued us from the dominion of darkness and brought us into the kingdom of the Son he loves, in whom we have redemption, the forgiveness of sins."
> —Colossians 1:13–14

Bible Study

"Who shall separate us from the love of Christ? Shall trouble or hardship or persecution or famine or nakedness or danger or sword? As it is written: 'For your sake we face death all day long; we are considered as sheep to be slaughtered.' No, in all these things we are more than conquerors through him who loved us. For I am convinced that neither death nor life, neither angels nor demons, neither the present nor the future, nor any powers, neither height nor depth, nor anything else in all creation, will be able to separate us from the love of God that is in Christ Jesus our Lord."
—Romans 8:35–39

Abortion to Mercy

"For God has given us a spirit of fear, but of power and of love and of a sound mind."
— 2 Timothy 1:7 NKJV

"You are the salt of the earth. But if the salt loses its saltiness, how can it be made salty again? It is no longer good for anything, except to be thrown out and trampled underfoot. 'You are the light of the world. A town built on a hill cannot be hidden."
—Matthew 5:13–14

"Being confident of this, that he who began a good work in you will carry it on to completion until the day of Christ Jesus."
—Philippians 1:6

Bible Study

"Therefore, there is now no condemnation for those who are in Christ Jesus, because through Christ Jesus the law of the Spirit who gives life has set you free from the law of sin and death."
—Romans 8:1–2

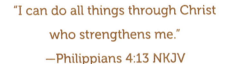

"I can do all things through Christ who strengthens me."
—Philippians 4:13 NKJV

Finally you are no longer a victim. Your trust, your obedience to Christ, your repentance, your love relationship with him has deemed you free. So now, you can say to God, "[I] trust in you; do not let me be put to shame, nor let my enemies triumph over me" (Psalm 25:2).

Our freedom is not a result of our own doing or our own will, but in having faith in Christ, giving our will over to him, surrendering our disappointment and unmet expectations of ourselves and others. In our agreement to surrender and in our ability to relinquish rights and die to ourselves, by faith we will continue to please him, love him, give honor to him, and serve him. For it is in dying that we live and find our freedom, and then he is able to live and move through us.[2]

A Prayer

Lord, forgive me for holding myself captive in guilt and shame. Forgive me for not seeing myself in the same beautiful way you see me. Please help me to work through this memory that I so desire to forget. Heal my heart of the wounds and scars. Help me to embrace the freedom you so long for me to have.

Jesus, I have lived with this secret and it has held me back from all I hope to do. Take it from me. I lay it at your feet and ask your precious blood to wash me clean forever.

Lord, tell my child I love him or her, and that one day we'll meet face to face so I can also ask my child's forgiveness. I am so very sorry for not giving my child a chance to come into this world.

Lord, most of all, help me to embrace this new journey of freedom, and not believe the lies the enemy will try to continue to accuse me with so that I remain in bondage to shame.

In Jesus' name, Amen.

And now, let the past be the past forever and ever always.

Chapter 3

Steps to Freedom

By Sharon Kay Ball, LPC-MHSP

Abortion is a controversial religious and political topic in our society, which creates a difficult environment for one to begin the healing process. For the purpose of your recovery, focusing on forgiveness and moving forward will allow you to begin that process of healing. Most women do not seek help from a counselor until 5–12 years after they have had an abortion. Typically this is because of the shame they feel combined with the "norm" in society to keep this a secret. This secret can lead to denial and suppression which can cause emotional harm to your body and soul.

Commit to Be Kind to Yourself

Be kind and gentle to yourself as you begin this process of healing. Sometimes your worst enemy can be you, and you in turn delay the start of your recovery. It is time to allow yourself to receive the gift of healing that only God can provide and only you can accept. You do deserve to experience peace within your heart.

Recognize that Grief Is Real

Grief is real after an abortion. Recovering from grief begins when the grief that has been kept secret is allowed to have a voice, when you allow it to have credibility—that is, when you let yourself experience the "movement" within your healing journey.

Often women will experience disenfranchised grief after an abortion. This is grief that is not given the right to mourn openly, although the experience of loss is very real. There is no social norm for grieving an abortion or ritual to acknowledge the pain you're going through. When your grief goes unrecognized or invalidated it will create an environment in which you feel "stuck." You may feel stuck in sadness, anger, apathy, or frustration. You may even have found a way to place it in a "box" where it will never be seen. This "box of heartache" reflects the captivity of your grief. Because it is disenfranchised grief, it is your box to carry alone. Society does not make it easy to grieve, so it is understandable that you want to hide this box.

Find a Support System

Seek professional help and support from friends who desire healing for you. If you do not have anyone you can trust, call a crisis pregnancy center in your town. They have individuals on staff who are trained and understand the grief and healing journey you are embarking on. Allow others to help you carry this box of heartache. The healing journey will be difficult and you will need support to grieve the loss of your baby.

Give Voice to Your Feelings

This part of your journey will be hard. I encourage you to meet with a qualified counselor to walk with you through your memories about your abortion. These sessions may be agonizing, and the support during this time will allow you to feel the vulnerability that comes when you remember the hard stuff. Denial and suppression of the grief are ineffective tools that allowed you to "keep going." However, the more you ignore that box of heartache, the more you empower the disenfranchised grief. Secret grief does not bring healing and restoration.

Secrets only carry power when they are kept secret! This will take courage, but may be a very empowering step for you to speak with someone about your story. Many women feel instant relief once they have shared about their abortion; the box of heartache feels lighter, as it should, now that you now have someone carrying it with you.

Healthy Grief

As you pay more attention to your grief and allow it to have a voice, you will notice many different emotions going on inside you at the same time: anger, relief, sadness, fear, and shame—just to name a few. This combination of emotions will create the feeling of confusion. But this is normal; this is grief, experiencing every emotion at the same time. Sometimes in life you must entertain the vast differences of emotions in your heart at the same time, knowing there is no way around them but to sit with them.

Forgiveness

There will come a time when you are faced with forgiving yourself. What will you do when the opportunity arises to forgive yourself? Will you ignore it and continue to use unhealthy behaviors to punish yourself? Behaviors like drinking, promiscuity, cutting, thoughts of suicide, belittling, or making yourself pay? Again allowing you to be your worst enemy?

Forgiveness will be hard, but it is necessary to healing. You cannot continue to carry this burden and punish yourself.

Your Spiritual Walk

It is important that through your recovery journey you take notice of where Jesus is during the process. Is he there beside you weeping with you? Or has he left you? Is he condemning you? Does Jesus take on the "societal norm" of expecting you to deal with your box of heartache alone? This is how Satan would want your spiritual walk to continue. However, through the healing and recovery process, you may begin to see that you have projected your shame and society's norm onto Jesus. You may discover that Jesus is and will always be with you. He hasn't left.

Notes:

1. Adapted from *Who I am in Christ* (Rose Publishing, 2010)

2. Adapted from *God Crazy Freedom* by Michelle Borquez (Carpenters Son Publishing, 2013)

OTHER BOOKS FROM THE FREEDOM SERIES

When divorce devastates a home, or a woman experiences abuse, paralyzing fear, abandonment, rape, or abortion, she needs God's restoration and wholeness. Michelle Borquez's **FREEDOM series** brings you true stories that show how to heal and experience joy again.

ABUSE TO FAVOR
When abuse happens, as women we tend to take on the pain alone. But you aren't alone and you don't have to deal with it alone. This book helps women understand that it's not your fault and you don't have to face it alone. Paperback, 4.5"x 6.5", 96 pages.

ABORTION TO MERCY
You never thought you would be in the situation of having an abortion and once it's over the pain is still there. But God has not left you because of this one action. This book helps you heal and move past the hurt. Paperback, 4.5"x 6.5", 96 pages.

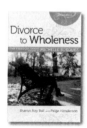

DIVORCE TO WHOLENESS
Divorce can tear you in half. It's not easy to deal with or sometimes even understand. With *Divorce to Wholeness* you learn how to put yourself back together and become whole again. Paperback, 4.5"x 6.5", 96 pages.

FEAR TO COURAGE
Fear to Courage shows women that they don't have to be a slave to their fears and helps them truly define their fears and develop the courage to move past them. This book shows women that through Christ all things are possible. Paperback, 4.5"x 6.5", 96 pages.

ABANDONMENT TO FORGIVENESS
At some point in every woman's life she has felt a sense of abandonment, for some this feeling is bigger than others. This book teaches women that no matter who has left you, God is always with you. Paperback, 4.5"x 6.5", 96 pages.

DECEIVED TO DELIVERED
She never thought she would cross the line and have an affair, but she did. *Deceived to Delivered* shows women how to strengthen their boundaries and restore their relationships. Paperback, 4.5"x 6.5", 96 pages.